For Emma and Hannah, spirited twins, and their mother, Marybeth.

Grateful acknowledgment to Chris Belden, panther expert, so generous with his time and expertise.
J. L.

Dedicated to all who help in conservation efforts.

Special thanks to Florida Fish and Wildlife Conservation Commission biologists Mark Lotz and
David Shindle for maps, advice, and arranging my wings over panthers.
P. M.

Library of Congress Cataloging-in-Publication Data

London, Jonathan, date.
Panther : shadow of the swamp / Jonathan London ;
illustrated by Paul Morin. — 1st U.S. ed.
p.   cm.
Summary: Words and pictures describe a night in the life
of a female Florida panther and her kittens.
ISBN 1-56402-623-X
1. Florida panther — Juvenile literature. [1. Florida panther.
2. Pumas. 3. Endangered species.] I. Morin, Paul, date, ill. II. Title.

QL737.C23 L66 2000
599.75'5 — dc21
99-086437

2 4 6 8 10 9 7 5 3 1

Printed in Belgium

This book was typeset in Tempus Sans. The illustrations were done in oils.

Candlewick Press
2067 Massachusetts Avenue
Cambridge, Massachusetts 02140

PANTHER
SHADOW OF THE SWAMP

Jonathan London illustrated by Paul Morin

CANDLEWICK PRESS
CAMBRIDGE, MASSACHUSETTS

The blinding heat of
summer quivers
above the swamp.

A long, thick tail
twitches in the saw grass.
A shadow flows.

It is panther.

She glides silently
and melts into the green
silence of the swamp.
It is dense with cypress,
gumbo limbo, strangler fig.

If you were a snowy egret
you would just catch a
glimpse of furred power
moving through the
saw palmetto.

Creatures scatter.
Snakes slither away.
Snapping turtles dive.
Alligator holds still,
eyes like periscopes.

Panther is hungry,
but more than hunger
drives her.

She pauses,
sniffs the bleached bones
of a white~tailed deer,
her favorite food.

The slightest sound,
panther's ears swivel.
The alligator's eyes drop
beneath the water's surface.

Panther sways her long
body and steps away
carefully, soundlessly,
with her huge paws.

She moves toward
drier ground.

She spots an armadillo.
Good food.
But panther needs more
now. Bigger prey.

The lucky armadillo
scurries beneath a stump.
A flock of white ibis swirls
up in the last light.

Time is running out.
It is dusk.
She has been on the hunt
since early morning.

Panther scouts the edge
of the grassy wetland,
choosing each step
through the slash pine.

A thick downpour
crashes into the
wet prairie . . .
then stops as quickly
as it started.
Fireflies flash.
Spanish moss drips.

Then panther senses
something else.
Something in the
steamy grass.

She crouches on her belly.
Creeps closer and closer.
Draws her hind paws
beneath her, and
extends her claws.

Then bursts forward
and pounces on a
wild hog.

It is over as quick and
furious as the short
summer storm.

Panther eats fast.
She has no time.
She covers the remains with
leaves and twigs.

Then glides back
through the watery wild.
Through the cypress swamp.
The vines hanging
like snakes.
The moonflowers.
The mist~haunted night.

To what awaits her.

To a great, uprooted
oak — her hidden den.

Where three spotted
blue-eyed kittens yowl,
attack their mother —
half in hunger,
half in play —
then fill their bellies
with mother's milk.

Panther is home again.

SOUTHERN FLORIDA

LAKE OKEECHOBEE

THE EVERGLADES

U.S.A.

The Everglades region of Florida, home to the last of the Florida panthers, is a unique and fragile ecosystem of interconnected lakes, rivers, and wetlands. The Florida panther, a subspecies of the western cougar or mountain lion, could once be found in large numbers from Texas to the Atlantic coast of the United States. Perhaps the last of the large cats east of the Mississippi River, only thirty to fifty panthers now live in the wilderness areas of southern Florida. These fierce predators are tender mothers, attentive and nurturing. There are usually two or three cubs in a litter, cared for by their mother. By eighteen months, the young panthers are well trained and can hunt and live on their own. While legally protected as an endangered species, these panthers are still threatened by the continuing loss of their habitat and by their own genetic deficiencies caused by crossbreeding within the small remaining population.